CONTENTS

A Christmas card posted from 5 Agden Road to Buffalo, America on December 18th 1908, detailing Edgehill Road, Montgomery Road, Oakdale Road, Union Road, St. Andrew's Church and Nether Edge Road.

Preface

"Old Sharrow and Nether Edge in Photographs" was the first book produced by the Nether Edge Neighbourhood Group Local History Section in 1985. It soon sold out. The Local History Section went on to publish several other books including "They Lived in Sharrow and Nether Edge" which was reprinted in 2000. To celebrate the 35th anniversary of the Nether Edge Neighbourhood Group, Christine Venables, their current chairman, has sought to reprint this book incorporating a few alterations /amendments.

Inevitably over the years there have been changes to some of the buildings which existed in 1985. The most obvious change is the demolition/ closure of Nether Edge Hospital, formerly the Ecclesall Bierlow Union Workhouse founded in 1843. The Hospital began to change in 1991 when the maternity services were transferred to the Jessop Hospital for Women. Gradually the other wards closed and in 1997 the main part of the Hospital was bought by Gleeson homes and converted to a gated housing complex. Some newer parts of the Hospital have been retained and the Cavendish wards together with the Lyndhurst block now form the Michael Carlisle Centre. Just the original main building of the Workhouse, being a Grade II listed building, remains facing Union Road. The old offices of the Ecclesall Union on Union Rd, which later became the Nether Edge Grammar School, have also been converted to apartments.

Another obvious change has been to the site of the old Bluecoat School, a listed building, on Psalter Lane. At the outbreak of the war the school was closed and the buildings requisitioned by the military for the Royal Army Service Corps. After the war, Sheffield Corporation took over responsibility for the premises first as an Emergency Training College and then as a College of Art. Various buildings were added to the site and in 1969 it became part of Sheffield Polytechnic and finally in 1992 part of Sheffield Hallam University. There will soon be further changes as Sheffield Hallam vacates the site in 2008 and plans are afoot for it to be developed as housing.

One area which has not changed is the house and grounds built by George Wostenholm on Kenwood Road. This is of particular interest as it forms the basis of the modern Nether Edge and Sharrow and their tree lined streets. Pages 17-19 detail George's work and his buying up of the local land. His many journeys to America are remembered in the local street names such as Boston Street and Washington Road and he named his house "Kenwood" after the Kenwood area near Oneida Lake in New York State. This is repeated in the names of nearby streets.

After George's death in 1876 his house and grounds was sold to Sheffield Refreshment Houses and became a temperance hotel. Over the years it has passed through several hotel chains and its names include Swallow Hotel and Marriott Hotel. It has recently become a Principal Hayley Hotel and renamed Kenwood Hall – another reminder of George Wostenholm. Nether Edge was declared a Conservation Area in 2002. This should help to ensure that any future developments are in keeping with its Victorian and Edwardian foundations and, hopefully, the preservation of its large gardens and trees.

Finally, we should mention the Picture Sheffield project at the Local Studies Library. Over 27,000 images from the Library collection have been scanned and catalogued. The website is www.picturesheffield.com and photographic quality prints can be ordered.

JOAN FLETT 2008

Foreword . . . *by Mary Walton*

I presume that I have been asked to write a foreword because I have already written about the neighbourhood and about Sheffield in general, though hardly enough to deserve the generous praise given to me by the authors of the introduction. It is true, I think, that I was the first to put the history of this neighbourhood in continuous narrative. I found it intensely interesting once I had begun it, and I am amazed, looking back, to remember that when we came to live in Clifford Road I was already twenty-one . . . and therefore might have been expected to have eyes in my head! I did not realise what an interesting area it was or how much of the old then remained. Anyone who in later years begins to notice or to understand his own locality is very lucky, because often it is only a happy chance which draws his eyes to antiquities in his own locality which are a cut above the Charles Peace type!

This booklet will, I think, be a happy chance to arouse interest in many of the people who buy it. Some readers will, I suppose, be people of advanced years who remember the actual scenes depicted. In young people, I hope, it will arouse a serious curiosity about the social and physical factors operating over the last century.

Looking through the booklet, I cannot help remembering the beginnings of this sort of work in the City Libraries, here acknowledged as a valuable source for material. When I was first appointed archivist in the Department of Local History (as it was called then) I was assistant to the Local Librarian, Miss Ethel Macdonald, to whom, amongst her other considerable duties, had been given the task of finding, acquiring, mounting and indexing pictures of old Sheffield. In those early days, they were stored in a single elderly wooden filing cabinet which smelled curiously of mushrooms. A tiny collection, but even then readers acknowledged its usefulness, and when Miss Macdonald left to be married she had laid the foundations on which, succeeding her as head of the department, I did my best to build. Appeals to the public from time to time produced an astonishing response in the way of gifts and loan of pictures, and today's fine collection now mounted, stored and copied with all modern aids, is an achievement to which many people have contributed: those who work in the department, the people who use the department, and those in the senior administration of the libraries, where there has always been someone to take an interest.

What has surprised me about the efforts of the local history group is how many pictures can still be found in private hands, and what rewarding work can be done by those outside professional bodies.

But perhaps this is all too personal, although if I don't tell you what I think I can't quite see why I'm writing this foreword!

All the essential material, all the essential information is given to you by the compilers of this booklet; it is my business to commend the work to you, which I do heartily.

* * *

Mary Walton in 'Fire-watching' garb. Central Library roof, sometime in World War Two.

Introduction

We started our Local History Group with talks by the acknowledged experts, Mary Walton and J. Edward Vickers, but later some people went on to find out more for themselves by using the excellent resources of the Central Library. Giles Robinson, who has had a lifelong interest in local history and who has made a special study of the buildings in our area, suggested that we should bring out a book of pictures which would illustrate the history of Sharrow and Nether Edge, and so inspired three more of us to join him in its production.

Before 1800 this was still largely a rural district. The village of Little Sheffield stood on the river Porter at Moorfoot, and straggled along the road to Heeley. Its open fields ran up the hillside to Sharrow Head, as far as the old trackway which we know today as Sharrow Lane and Psalter Lane. Two other hamlets, Cherry Tree Hill and Machon Bank, each consisted of a handful of farms and houses belonging to small craftsmen and agricultural workers. Little Sheffield Grange and the Priory Barn still stood on Sharrow Lane, a reminder that in medieval times much of the land in these parts belonged to Worksop Priory. The farms of Upper Edge, Nether Edge and Edge End occupied most of the land on both sides of Brincliffe Edge as far as Banner Cross Hall. Along the rivers Porter and Sheaf ran strings of dams, with many small water-powered industries. Up on Brincliffe Edge were the sandstone quarries which were to provide the building material for most of our houses.

In the early years of the nineteenth century wealthy Sheffield merchants and manufacturers began to build their houses up on our hillsides, away from the smoke and grime of the city. George Wostenholm of Kenwood Park played the most important part in the development of this pleasant middle-class suburb when he laid out the tree-lined roads of the Kenwood Estate, and later, with Thomas Steade, the area round Crescent Road and Chippinghouse Road. The Montgomery Land Society bought up large sections of land on the Brincliffe hillside, and sold off plots on which arose large and small stone villas. In late Victorian and Edwardian times came the rows of terrace houses which completed the conversion of open countryside to city suburb. Recent years have seen the building of small houses and blocks of flats, many of them in the gardens of Victorian villas or on the sites of houses damaged in the blitz.

All this has left us with a district whose remarkable variety, both in its buildings and in its people, is one of the chief attractions of life in present-day Nether Edge and Sharrow. We have tried to include pictures which illustrate many different aspects of the way our area has developed over the last century and a half, though we have been limited by what we could find and by our wish not to use pictures which have often appeared in other books. Sometimes the interest of a subject has led us to include a picture whose technical quality leaves much to be desired.

Our thanks are due first and foremost to Mary Walton, whose books especially "A History of the Parish of Sharrow", have been our inspiration and our major source of information. She is the professional, and we are only amateurs. Martin Olive and the staff of the Local History and Archives Departments at the Central Library have given us much help and encouragement, and their collections have been the source of many of our pictures. The Nether Edge Neighbourhood Group has provided the funds, without which we could not have undertaken this venture, and many local people have lent us their pictures and given us information. To all of them we say a heartfelt thank you.

* * *

Shirley Meek, Jackie Hamilton, Giles Robinson, Malcolm Weston.
May, 1985.

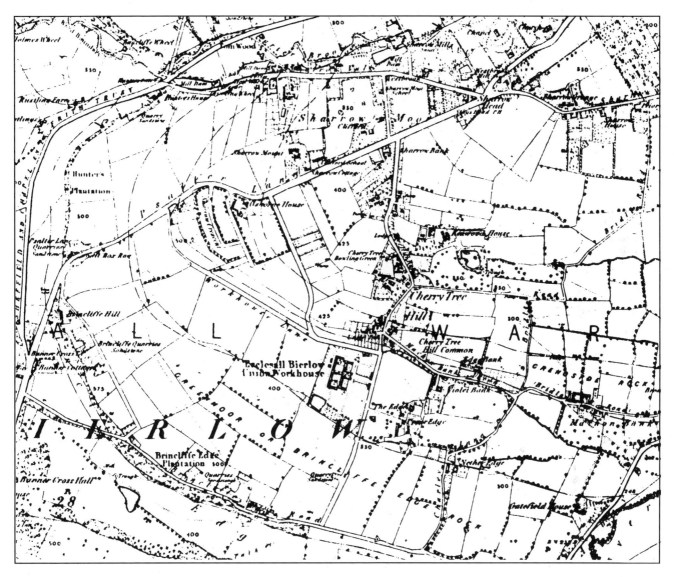

The area as it was in 1855. The major roads are beginning to appear but very little building has taken place at this date. The older settlements such as Machon Bank, Nether and Upper Edge and Cherry Tree Hill can still be identified on this map, whilst George Wostenholm's Kenwood and the Union Workhouse have just been built.

Machon Bank: First mentioned in medieval times as Hawslin Bank, this small hamlet consisting of just a few farms stood between Joshua and Emily Roads underneath the present Machon Bank highway.

The later name came from the Machon family who lived here in the 16th century. Other occupants were the Sheldons, commemorated by Sheldon Road for which planning permission was given to the second Montgomery Land Society in 1877. Much of the land on the north side of Machon Bank was developed by the trustees of a local landowner, William Spooner, and this included Joshua and Emily Roads named after members of the Spooner family.

The old hamlet was demolished to make way for the new development around the year 1903. This is taking place in the second photograph.

Cherry Tree Cottages: Cherry Tree Lane wound over Cherry Tree Common, from Sharrow Moor towards Nether Edge. This group of early eighteenth century cottages stood on its west side at Cherry Tree Hill. Sadly, they were demolished in the late 1960s. Fortunately the nearby seventeenth century house, known as the Bowling Green Inn in Victorian times but later named Roadside, still stands on Cherry Tree Road today.

This picture shows the house belonging to Cherrytree Farm. It stood on Cherry Tree Lane at right angles to the present Machon Bank Road, opposite the Union Hotel. The farmhouse was occupied by the Ludlam family & may have been built by them in the mid - 1600s. A sketch made in 1907 tells that "TL 1658" & "GL" were carved on opposite gable ends. It is likely that these inscriptions refer to a Thomas & a George Ludlam, but it is impossible to say precisely which members of the family have been recorded. When Robert Savage, a cutler, took over part of the property, it became two dwellings. He added his own initials & the date of 1673 to the lintel over the main entrance doorway. Robert combined farming with the cutlery trade and it remained in the Savage family. Robert's grandson, the Rev. Thomas Savage, lived there until his death in 1782. The last tenant of Cherry Tree Farm was Mr. Ibbotson, shown here, who occupied it until 1906. The house was then demolished, so that building could take place on Meadow Bank Avenue.

5

The Edge: originated as an outbuilding to the Upper Edge Farmhouse, but the building we can see today was constructed in the late 18th century by Joseph Badger, a Sheffield architect who is best known for Renishaw Hall.

From 1841 to 1873 Thomas Rawson Barker lived at the Edge. He was the youngest ever Mayor of Sheffield, Chairman of the Ecclesall Board of Guardians and a noted cricketer who once bowled out an all-England eleven in an hour. After he died the gardens of the Edge were sold for building, and Barkers Road is on part of this land. The house still stands on Ladysmith Avenue and, after a sad period of delapidation, has recently been restored to something approaching its former state.

Nether Edge: This building was originally a farmhouse called Nether Edge to distinguish it from another farm, Upper Edge, which stood between Fountside Flats and Edgebrook Road. The history of Nether Edge goes back at least as far as medieval times. The lands stretched up the hillside towards Brincliffe Edge, and in 1853 they were bought for building purposes by the Sheffield Reform Freehold Benefit Building Society. Development was delayed for some time but got under way in the 1860s. The farm became a public house, with a bowling green and a public tea-garden. Part of the original stonework of the farmhouse can still be seen from Oakhill Road.

Archer Field: was a medieval farm which was completely rebuilt and slightly re-sited between 1850 and 1860 by the landlord, John Rodgers of Abbeydale House. It was again rebuilt as a large villa in the Tudor Gothic style, together with a gatehouse facing Archer Lane, by about 1870, and both these buildings can be seen in the background of this picture. Archer House, as the villa was known, lasted until 1933 when it was sold for demolition, and a housing estate was built on its remaining land bounded by Carterknowle Road, Bannerdale Road and Archer Lane. In the foreground of the photo is Jennings Farm. It was built about 1800, to make use of 10 acres of land which were originally part of the Edge End estate. Although the farm out-buildings were demolished early this century, the house itself still stands and was for a long time the home of Mr. and Mrs. Jennings, who ran a general shop there. More recently alterations and renovation have removed something of the period feel this place once had.

Archer Lane: was part of an ancient bridleway which led from Holt House Farm over Brincliffe Edge and down Charley Lane (now Oakhill Road) to the farm called Nether Edge (now the Brincliffe Oaks Hotel). After that the ways branched — one went left to Cherry Tree Hill, and the other across the fields to Sharrow Lane and on to Sheffield. In this view, Jennings' Farm is visible at the bottom of the hill, with open country beyond, and the high wall on the left enclosed the grounds of Edge End. This was an old farm which dated back to medieval times, and it stood more or less where the Scout hut is now. The large stones on the right were there mainly to prevent carts eroding the bank side, but also provided a brake into which the wheels of the cart could be wedged while the horse had a rest. The steps up to the field are still there, albeit in a rather decrepit state.

Archer House Gatehouse: This picture shows the gatehouse to Archer House. It is still standing in Archer Lane, opposite the ends of Struan Road and Glentilt Road, but the surroundings are now very different.

9

Knab Farm: A delightful study of Knab Farm taken in the 1930s — a few years before its demolition. It was owned latterly by the Denniff family (of butchery fame) and stood approximately where the Cherry Tree Inn now stands on Carterknowle Road. Knab Farm Estate, built in the 1950s, was named after it. The houses in the background are on Bincliffe Edge Road.

Banner Cross Hall: The drawing of Banner Cross Hall reproduced here comes from the field measurement book of William Fairbank, surveyor, dated 1757. It shows the sixteenth century building which had earlier belonged to the Brights. Members of this extensive family owned land all over the Sheffield district, notably at Carbrook Hall in Attercliffe, but also at Upper and Nether Edge. Early in the nineteenth century the old hall was replaced by the present Gothic Revival building designed by Sir Jeffrey Wyatville, the architect who remodelled Windsor Castle in 1824. It now houses the firm of Henry Boot and Sons.

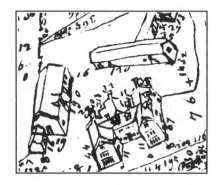

Brincliffe Edge Road: is one of the oldest thoroughfares in the area — its use as a bridleway goes back to medieval times. Note the very fine traffic island (which remained until the early 1950s) and the 'sewer gas lamp' in the background. These were used to burn off any methane gas which collected in the sewers and a still-operative example can be found at the top of Union Road.

Brincliffe Edge: This is the end of Brincliffe Edge Road just before Knab Farm Estate was built in the 1950s. Prior to that time, Bannerdale Road terminated in a field about half way up and there was just a track up to the point shown in the photograph. The grazing rights to this part of Brincliffe Edge were rented by the Vallé family who had a small-holding on Sharrow Vale Road until the late 1950s.

Sharrow Head House: This picture shows Sharrow Head House which was built about 1760 for William Battie, a Sheffield attorney, apparently to the designs of the architect Platt of Rotherham, who also designed Mount Pleasant for the Sitwells. The eighteenth century building adjoined an older house dating from 1664, in which William Battie's father had lived, but this seventeenth century wing was demolished about 1900.

Many Georgian buildings in Sheffield became temporary homes for Victorian gentlemen who were coming up in the world, before they aspired to their own purpose-built villas. Henry Vickers, a solicitor, rented Sharrow Head in the 1850s until he moved into his own house, Holmwood, in Ecclesall.

The Georgian part of Sharrow Head House still stands today although most of its once extensive grounds were lost when land was sold off to build houses on Cemetery Road, Sharrow Lane and Grange Crescent Road.

Sharrow Head: The large house which is now a nursing home was just being completed for Mr. Charles Parkins, surgeon and dentist when this photo was taken in 1907. All the windows are open to allow new plasterwork to dry out. Were the crowds on Sharrow Lane going to a football match at Bramall Lane? Perhaps someone can tell us.

"The Priory": The building in this picture stood off the north side of Priory Road exactly beneath the terrace of Priory Avenue. It was called The Priory because the site was that of Little Sheffield Grange, established in the twelfth century by the monks of Worksop Priory. This institution was responsible for turning a lot of uncultivated land in the Sharrow district into farmland but was dissolved in 1538. The central section and the left wing of the building were probably built in the 15th and 16th centuries.

"Sharrow Priory": This fine seventeenth century house in Sharrow Lane bore the initials and date 'GL 1633', which stood for George Lee who died in 1649. It survived into the late nineteenth century, last appearing in the directory for 1887, but was sadly demolished to make way for the school room of Sharrow St. John's Methodist Church.

Abbeydale House: In 19th century Sheffield, the most famous cutlery firm was that of Joseph Rodgers and Sons. The company's success was largely due to the founder's enterprising son John Rodgers. In 1849 John built himself a new house of polished Anston stone in the Italian style of architecture, to the designs of Rooke Harrison. He died ten years later, and his nephew Robert Newbould took over the running of the business. Newbould built himself a house a little further up the Abbeydale Road in 1851, perhaps using the same architect, and called it Abbeydale Grange. Both houses still stand, Abbeydale Grange being part of the comprehensive school of the same name.

Snowite Laundry: Abbeydale House was taken over between 1903 and 1906 by the Snowite Laundry, founded by Mr. W. Bryars. This picture dates from about 1929, and shows the well-equipped transport system belonging to Snowite Ltd. These are Morris Oxford vans. In the foreground is Abbeydale Road, and the vans are standing in Barmouth Road. At this time Abbeydale House was the laundry's registered offices and administrative department, the company's boardroom being on the first floor. Until quite recently the building was empty, but is now an antiques warehouse.

Chipping House: Chipping House, whose site was to the west of Brookfield Road, was built by John Shortridge an important figure in Victorian Sheffield. He became a sub-contractor in the firm of Blackie and Shortridge who built the Wicker viaduct and he also ran a steel business called Shortridge Howell & Co.

Chipping House was built about 1851 to the designs of the architect T.F. Cashin and was named after Chipping in Lancashire where, in 1826, Shortridge had married Ellen Leach. Shortridge began to develop the Chipping House Estate for housing before his death in 1869. His memorial is in Heeley Churchyard. The office block of Shortridge Howell & Co., built in 1853, still dominates The Wicker, and may also have been designed by T.F. Cashin.

Chippinghouse Road: This is an Edwardian picture of Upper Chippinghouse Road. The houses here were built almost entirely by Thomas Steade during the 1870s. The road was originally called Shortridge Road, and had probably been laid out as early as 1853 by John Shortridge of Chipping House. Steade, who lived at Chipping House himself for a time, was originally an iron-founder but became involved in building by 1860. He first worked in co-operation with George Wostenholm, building houses in Montgomery Road, Kenwood Park Road, Crescent Road and Wostenholm Road. Later he began to lay out and develop on his own account Steade Road, Albany Road, and St. Ronan's Road amongst others in our district, with many streets in Attercliffe and other parts of Sheffield as well. He also ran the Brincliffe, Nether Edge and Sharrow Omnibus Company, in competition with the trams.

Lower Bannerdale Road: This row of houses in lower Bannerdale Road was built by James Wilkinson about 1903. James and his father had been building in the Heeley and Sharrow districts since the 1870s. As well as the Bannerdale Road development, James was responsible for the houses on the lower half of Carterknowle Road, Edgedale Road and portions of Abbeydale Road. Nearer the centre of Nether Edge he almost certainly built a substantial part of Sheldon Road.

George Wostenholm: was the son of a Sheffield cutler who followed his father into the family business. He bought the Washington Works in Wellington Street, extended them and built up a very profitable concern. Much of their trade was with the United States, to which George made frequent visits. They made the famous Bowie knives, as supplied to James Bowie of Alamo fame, as well as the IXL table knives.

Wostenholm started to buy land off Cherry Tree Lane in 1836, and by 1849 the architectural firm of Flockton and Son had built him a splendid house which he called Kenwood. It stood in a large park which was laid out by Robert Marnock, the landscape gardener who had planned the Botanical Gardens. This picture shows Kenwood as it was in 1853.

KENWOOD NEAR SHEFFIELD.

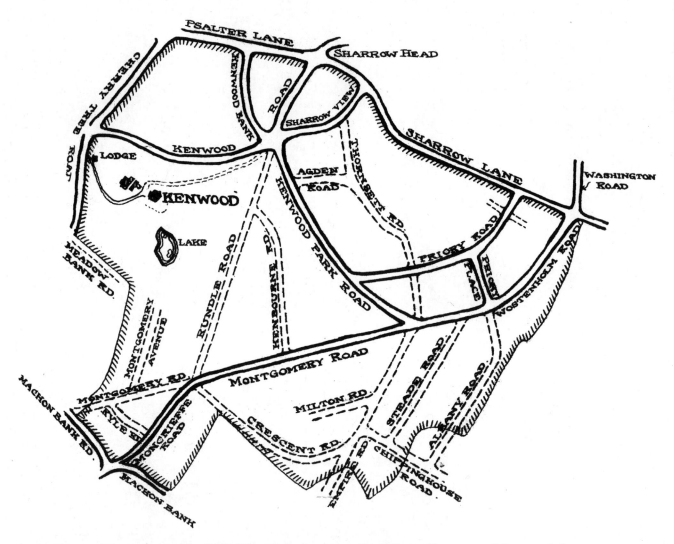

Kenwood Estate: During the 1850s Wostenholm bought up land all over Sharrow until he owned almost everything from Sharrow Head to Brincliffe Edge and down to the Abbeydale Road. With Robert Marnock and Thomas Steade the builder he laid out the estate for development as a middle class residential area. The houses were to be substantial gentlemen's residences, and their deeds still forbid ungentlemanly activities such as soap boiling and the keeping of tea gardens! This sketch dated 1928 shows the original Kenwood estate with modern roads added in dotted lines

Croquet Party: Many Sheffield notables were visitors at Kenwood, including the poet James Montgomery. This picture of a croquet party on the lawn at Kenwood must have been taken not long before George Wostenholm's death in 1876, at the age of 74. He stands behind the table between his third wife and her sister, Miss Rundle.

"It's mine - all mine!" The gentleman displaying such obvious proprietorial satisfaction is Mr. Richard Paul Fisher, the manager of an iron foundry, who lived at 58 Brincliffe Edge Road from the 1890s until well into the 1920s. The horse and trap have obviously just been brought out of the stable for the photographer's benefit; the passenger is undoubtedly Mrs. Sarah Ann Fisher. Both the house and the stable still stand at the junction of Edge Hill Road and Brincliffe Edge in a very well preserved and virtually unchanged condition.

Edge Hill Road: This house on Edge Hill Road was built for William Singleton, a cutlery manufacturer, about 1875. The two houses shown on this page were built on plots sold by the Montgomery Land Society.

All the larger houses in Nether Edge would have had a staff of several domestic servants, and even the smaller ones would have had at least one "general". Hours of work were long, pay was very small, and the girls proudly showing off the young master in this picture would have been lucky to have one half-day off each week.

The Montgomery Oaks: Two views of the Montgomery Oaks, two ancient trees of tremendous girth which stood at the junction of Oakdale Road and Oakhill Road. They were greatly admired by James Montgomery, the poet and editor of the Sheffield Iris. The trees were cut down in the First War and were lucky to last that long. In 1874 the Secretary of the Montgomery Land Society was writing to George Wostenholm saying that the committee proposed to "cut down two old oak trees in Oakdale Road because the lots would not sell with the trees there". Wostenholm was offered first refusal at 30/- (£1.50) each, but ignored the offer. Arboreal experts might like to tell us whether the drawing and the photograph show the same tree at different ages or whether each portrays a different tree.

The Bowling Club: The Nether Edge Proprietary Bowling Club was founded in 1867. Its first president was Councillor Benjamin Staniforth, a silver plater, who had settled at 13 Byron Road in 1865. With other solid citizens of the neighbourhood, he set up this club which was to provide (in the words of a later member) "primarily for the Game of Bowls, and secondly a rendezvous where gentlemen may meet for other amusements".

The bowling green was, and is, one of the largest in Yorkshire and has seen many memorable matches. The other amusements included billiards, for which a large saloon was built on the first floor of the club house, card games such as solo, loo and nap, and later the new game of ping-pong.

The staid and respectable-looking gentlemen in our pictures could also do their share of drinking. Early minute books list regular orders for "one cask of beer, one cask of whisky and two dozen bottles of claret"; from time to time they also recorded altercations between members and other disorderly behaviour. The club survived these upheavals, together with those caused by the stinking smoke from the Tramway depot next door, financial crises and air raid damage in 1940. It continues to flourish 118 years after its foundation.

Sharrow Cycling Club: Cycling in Sheffield really began in 1872, when the Sheffield Bicycling Club opened its training ground in Sharrow Vale. Here for the price of 6d. novices could have their first taste of the joys of mounting a 52″ wheel "ordinary", or penny farthing, and wobbling off alongside (or sometimes into) the Porter Brook. In 1887 four lads from Sharrow, all keen cyclists, met at the bottom of Rundle Road and decided to form the Sharrow Cycling Club which is still very much alive today.

This picture shows a group of Club stalwarts outside their headquarters at the old Pomona Hotel in Ecclesall Road in the 1890s. Who said that B.M.X. bikes were a recent craze?

Here is the start of one of the Club's famous track races at Bramall Lane, which brought in huge crowds of spectators. Note Richdale's Brewery in the background. The track had square corners, and as the Cricket Club complained bitterly of damage to their pitch if the cyclists used too many cinders for banking them up, cycle racing at 'The Lane' could be fairly dangerous.

Wostenholm Road: A horse tram thunders its way to Nether Edge terminus about 1895. The lines for horse trams were laid by Sheffield Corporation in the 1880s and leased to the then privately owned Sheffield Tramways Company who ran their own horse trams. At Nether Edge - one of the earliest horse tram routes - the trams were kept overnight in the building which is now Machon Bank Garage (and previously a Kenning's petrol station) whilst the horses were stabled in Byron Road.

In 1896, the corporation took over the whole tramway system and electrification commenced almost immediately. The Tinsley to Nether Edge route was the first to be completed in 1899 when an inauguration run by a convoy of trams laden with civic dignitories took place on September 5th. The 500 volt DC current to operate the system was generated at Kelham Island - now an industrial museum - until trams were discontinued in the 1960s. The Nether Edge trams ran until July 1934 when buses took over.

Nether Edge Market: The butcher's and the baker's (built in 1880) at the terminus about 1910. It would be nice to see the plant troughs and hanging baskets again - but the sides of meat are probably better in the fridge! Across Nether Edge Road, the present sweet shop has not yet been built on to the end of Ashland House.

Tram Terminus, Nether Edge: Open-topped tram No. 18 and its crew
stand at the terminus waiting for the exact time of departure to Sheffield.
The tram routes were originally identified by their initials (hence N.E. for
Nether Edge) and 'modesty boards' were fitted to upper decks to hide the
ankles of ladies bold enough to ride on top. The boards were used to
carry advertising at different periods but this particular tram appears to
have blank boards. The ornate wire support standards can be clearly seen
here; originally they were smartly painted in black and green with a gold
'star'.

Shirle Hill: The core of Shirle Hill was built in 1809. This was a small Georgian house, and is the part on the far right of this picture. For a time this was the home of John Brown, who founded the firm of John Brown and Co. Ltd., the largest steel making business in Sheffield's history. In 1862 the prime minister, Lord Palmerston, visited Brown here to discuss arms manufacture. Brown built himself a large mansion called Endcliffe Hall in 1864, and his managing director William Bragge moved into Shirle Hill. In 1865 Bragge got permission to extend the building. He added the larger left wing and refronted the older house, leaving the structure seen in the photograph.

Belgian Refugees: When the German armies swept across Belgium in August 1914, thousands of refugees fled to Britain. In September the first Belgian refugees arrived in Sheffield and were taken to the reception centre at Shirle Hill. The early arrivals were peasants from Louvain, but after the fall of Antwerp in October many more refugees from that city flooded into Sheffield. By mid-November nearly 800 had arrived. As well as 90 still at Shirle Hill, there were others at the Workhouse in Union Road, at the Wilson's Westbrook House, and even a family of eight with Miss Kenny, a schoolteacher, in Priory Terrace. It would be four years before they could go home.

The Workhouse: The Ecclesall Union Workhouse was opened in 1843. Earlier, the poor of Ecclesall Parish had been housed at Sharrow Mount on Psalter Lane but this had become too small for the growing population. The Board of Guardians bought land in 1839, and employed William Flockton to design buildings which would take 500 inmates. They included the old and infirm, orphan children, the chronic sick, lunatics and vagrants. Workhouse life was hard, and families were separated on entry, so poor people did all they could to avoid being sent there.

The Kitchen: Over the years the Union expanded and the system became more humane. A maternity block opened in 1897, and in 1903 the children were moved to cottage homes at Lodge Moor. From 1929 onwards the Workhouse became known as Nether Edge Hospital. This picture shows the kitchens some time in the 1920s. We have tried and failed to find out more about Mrs. Warris (marked with X). Can anyone help us?

The Union Hotel: was built early in the 1840s, presumably to cater for the thirst of the workers on the new Ecclesall Union Workhouse which was going up down the road. The first recorded landlord was Joseph Boote, who kept the hotel from 1845 to 1871. This picture, taken in Edwardian times, also shows the cab rank at the top of Machon Bank Road.

It was common practice for cabbies to stand outside 'quality' pubs in the hope of getting a fare - whilst no doubt fortifying themselves with liquid refreshment. Local cabs were owned by Haigh's or Reuben Thompson's, whose old livery stables at Havelock Bridge, Queen's Road, have recently been demolished.

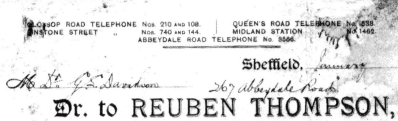

Billhead: One of Reuben Thompson's accounts to a Dr. Davison who practised at 267 Abbeydale Road and used a cab for several hours daily - presumably for his sick round. At this time (1906), a hansom cab was a mere two shillings (10p) per hour whilst a trip to and from the Lyceum was only three shillings.

Brincliffe Rise: Just up the hill from the Ecclesall Union Workhouse, life was very different for the comfortable middle class inhabitants of Brincliffe Rise. A pair of large semi-detached houses, now demolished to make way for a block of flats, was built in the 1850s at the top of Osborne Road, or Workhouse Lane as it was called then. As this picture shows, the Edwardian residents lived in some style and could afford to keep three maid servants as well as a rabbit.

Audrey Cottage: in Union Road, was another early villa built in Nether Edge. We believe that it was designed and built about 1845 by William Flockton, architect of the Union Workhouse and of George Wostenholm's Kenwood.

The 1876 directory gives the house's occupant as Mrs. Rundle, and the 1879 directory gives George Edward Rundle, M.B. These must have been relatives of George Wostenholm's third wife, Eliza Maria Rundle, and were probably her mother and brother.

Westbrook Mill: The rear view of Westbrook Mill, originally owned by a break-away part of the Wilson family who still own Sharrow Mills. Locally, the two snuff mills were always known as Top Mill and Bottom Mill. In more recent times, Westbrook Mill became part of the Wills tobacco empire.

Sharrow Mills: Wilson's Snuff Mill as it has looked since 1737. Originally it produced a wide range of goods before concentrating on snuff which is still produced to this day, largely by the original machinery. Although the water operated equipment is still in good working order, it is used less frequently nowadays because "the vibration makes the tiles fall off the roof". It is a tribute to the Wilson Family and the present incumbent - Mr. Mark Chaytor - that this unique industrial relic is preserved in such fine condition.

The Wilsons: Three generations of Wilsons at Stanedge Lodge in 1885. Despite their benevolence and generosity, the Wilsons were a bloodthirsty lot, firing off at almost anything that moved and keeping the most immaculate records of their kills.

Wilson's Wall: The boundary wall to Wilson's site on Sharrow Vale Road. The groove was worn by generations of small boys (and girls) walking on top of the wall. Flats are now built in the paddock to the right of the wall and the groove has been obscured by additional coping stones. Typically, Wilsons have preserved a small length of the wall in their works.

Frog Walk: Originally marking the boundary between Sharrow Moor and farmland belonging to Broom Hall, Frog Walk is an old footpath from Sharrow Head to Stalker Lees. Some authorities think that the name stems from the nickname of the adjoining footway - Stalker Walk. This was known as the Old Walk - or in Sheffield dialect "T' owd Walk", or Toad Walk. The association of frog with toad is obvious but a more likely explanation is the number of frogs once found on this dark and damp patch which runs from Westbrook millpond to the Porter Brook.

The Stag: The Stag Hotel on Psalter Lane was built in 1805 by the Rev. Alexander Mackenzie, to replace a delapidated alehouse which had stood in front of his house at Sharrow Head. The original name was The Stag's Head from the Mackenzie crest. Coaches and wagons called here on their way to Buxton and Chapel by the turnpike road which led from Sheffield along the moor to Highfields, and then up Sharrow Lane and Psalter Lane to Ringinglow. At the side of the Inn were large stables which were only demolished a few years ago.

Sharrow Vale Cottages: The cottages in the first photo still stand on the lower side of Sharrow Vale Road, close to the River Porter. The white building is certainly as old as 1757 when it was known as Wainwright's Cottage, but the other was built early in the nineteenth century.

The second photo shows four cottages which stood on the opposite side of Sharrow Vale Road, at the bottom of Jarrow Road. They were also built early in the 1800s. Most of these buildings would have housed employees of the three water-driven works on the Porter. Wilson's Snuff Mill remains, but the other two have gone. The Upper Lescar Wheel (just below Hunter's Bar) and the Nether Lescar Wheel (by the Porter Cottage public house) were both originally grinding wheels. The firm of Samuel Cocker & Son took over the Nether Lescar site for a forge and tilt in the 1830s and later expanded their works to make wire, needles, pins, fish hooks etc.

Sharrow Vale Road: Sharrow Vale Road has changed only little since this photograph was taken in the early 1920s. The man on the cart is one of the Vallé family who had a smallholding on the site which is now Hadfield's Garage. Just behind the hoardings was a small area known as 'the Piggy' where everyone dumped their rubbish.

The 'Tin Chapel': The Wycliffe Church Mission on Hickmott Road almost deserves a separate history of its own. Its origins began in the old school house on Bagshot Street and the present 'tin chapel' was finished in 1902 with a seating capacity of 300. The leading light of the mission was the Rev. F. Vince (known as 'Daddy' Vince) who was still living at 37 Bingham Park Crescent as late as 1941. Someone who remembers the early days says "He was an Old Testament prophet-like man who used to buy or beg cheap groceries from local shops and then distribute them to the poor in return for their attendance at the Mission.

Brooke Bray's Shop: Here are Brooke Bray's house and shop on Sharrow Vale Road about 1890. The adjoining houses are being converted into shops in the photograph, and it can be seen that there are no further buildings all the way to Hunter's Bar. The houses in the distance on the left are in Junction Road. Behind Brooke Bray's, the Upper Lescar Dam stretched to the Ecclesall Road.

Hunter's Bar: The actual tolls at Hunter's Bar were abolished in October 1884 - shortly after this photograph was taken. Reuben Thompson's horse bus is in attendance, together with the local constabulary. The gate posts (which were moved to the entrance of Endcliffe Park) were replaced in their original position in the 1960s.

Mr. Slater's Cars: These splendid cars belonged to Mr. Leonard Slater, who moved to Spring Leigh on Rundle Road in 1912 and lived there for more than forty years. The two on the left are a 1914 Sheffield Simplex Landaulette and a 1914 Sheffield Simplex tourer - both Sheffield-made cars. Earl Fitzwilliam, who owned the Simplex firm, always vetted prospective customers personally to see if they were suitable persons to drive his cars! The chassis cost £695; the customer would then have a body built on it to suit his taste. The car on the right is a Straker-Squire of similar vintage.

Laycock Car: A Charron-Laycock car at the works in Archer Lane, Millhouses, 1919. The Charron-Laycock was an exceptionally well engineered car built to a French design by the W.S. Laycock Co. in 1919 and 1920. It did well in competitions and the man in the photograph was a French racing driver - a M. Pradier - employed as the official 'works' driver. In spite of its short production span, the car was popular with the nobility and gentry. Dame Ellen Terry bought one and novelist Dennis Wheatley ordered one but cancelled when the price rose by a third overnight! 500 cars had been produced before the W.S. Laycock Co. went into liquidation in 1920 and a further 200 were built up from spare parts by Gower & Lee of London. A beautifully restored example may be seen in the reception office of the Archer Road factory.

The Richardson Car: A typical week's production at the Richardson Car Factory, Finbat Works, Aizlewood Road. The cars were built in an old brickworks and were typical of the 'cyclecars' which enjoyed a brief boom after the first world war. Several hundred of this model were made until production ceased in 1922; the car had a V-twin air cooled J.A.P. engine in 8hp and 10hp sizes and was unusual in having a crude form of infinitely variable transmission.

Mr. Richardson lived in a large house on Sharrow View until his death a few years ago and one of the two surviving cars is on show at Kelham Island Industrial Museum.

Mrs. Richardson (who won a Brooklands Medal in this car) with her mother on a lane at the side of the works. This was approximately at the end of Hale Street where the old footpath still runs down to Broadfield Road. Note the extra large steering wheel which could be fitted to ladies' cars to lighten the otherwise heavy steering.

Smeaton Terrace: was built by a local builder, John Dawson Cook, in 1886. This picture was taken just prior to the first world war and before the two houses past the sun blind had been converted into shops and the raised paved area extended. The nearest shop was, at the time of this photograph, a butcher, the next a fruiterer, then a draper and finally Johnson Brothers Dyers Ltd. Note the ubiquitous errand boy, now extinct.

Sharrow Lane: Sharrow Lane photographed about 1910. There are many subtle differences to be seen when the present day view is compared to this picture. At the time of this picture the shop on the corner was the premises of John Glew, confectioner. The actual terrace of which it is a part was built in 1878 by John Wilkinson of The Priory. (See page 13).

The back of Priory Terrace built about 1860 is visible on the right. The terraced houses across the road went up in the 1870s.

Sharrow St. John's: This is believed to be the opening ceremony at St. John's, Sharrow Lane in 1905. The name 'Sharrow St. John's' was the result of the amalgamation of St. John's Chapel, John Street and Sharrow Street Chapel. The shop on the extreme left is Wainwright's drapers and haberdashers who later moved to Heeley Bottom and were still in business until relatively recently. The shop later became a branch of Davy's the bakers, until its demolition in the 1960s. The stone house on the right, Rock House, was built for Nathaniel Pearson, medical practitioner, about 1861 as part of George Wostenholm's Kenwood development.

"Setting Out": In 1920, Sharrow Lane Boys' School had a week's outing to Wentworth, sleeping in the outhouses of Wentworth House - then still the seat of the Fitzwilliam family. The cost of the whole week was a mere 2/6 (12½p)! The photograph is taken outside Sharrow St. John's schoolroom and the charabanc belongs to Caudles who are still in the haulage business at Queen's Road. The Caudle family were founder-members of Sharrow St. John's and are still active in it.

Sharrow Lane: Here is Sharrow Lane about the beginning of this century, looking towards Sharrow Head from the end of Grange Crescent. Sharrow Grange was still standing behind the wall on the right, as it had done since before 1756 when the surveyor Fairbanks noted it as a farm with four fields. The house was sold to Sheffield Corporation in 1928 to be used for the welfare of the blind, and after the present Blind Workshops had been built in 1930 it was demolished so that Sharrow Lane could be widened. Grange Crescent and Grange Road were laid out for one of Sharrow Grange's occupants the brewer Thomas Marrian, about 1872.

Old School House: Sharrow Moor Endowed School stood in what is now Bagshot Street. The nearer part was built in 1668, and it was renovated and extended in 1769. It had an endowment of £5 a year, to teach 12 free pupils reading and writing, but fee-paying pupils were taught as well. The school flourished under headmaster "Daddy" Whitehead, in charge from 1865 to 1890. He loved music, and was choirmaster at St. Mark's, Broomhill. After he died and Hunter's Bar Board School opened, pupil numbers fell and the new headmaster had to take another job and leave his wife to do the teaching. The school closed and was demolished in 1904.

Clifford School: In 1832 Joseph Wilson, of the Snuff Mill family, gave some land from the grounds of his house, Clifford, on Psalter Lane as well as the money to build a school for the neighbourhood. Clifford First School is still an essential part of Sharrow today. It became a National School, and after 1869 a Church School attached to St. Andrew's but also under the Sheffield School Board. The buildings we see today mostly date from 1896, when the original school was extended with the help of another legacy from the Wilsons.

Miss Slater: One of Clifford School's best loved headmistresses was Miss Annie Slater. She ran the school firmly and kindly for 34 years, from 1894 when she first took charge to 1928 when she died a few months after retiring through ill health. A typical inspector's comment is found in the school log book for 1897: "The children are kindly handled and in very good order, and the results of instruction in class subjects are very creditable".

Arnold Loosemore: Sheffield's only V.C., was the youngest of seven brothers all educated at Clifford School. His elder brothers enlisted in 1914, and he soon managed to join them in the Army by giving a false age. He first distinguished himself by shooting down a German plane with his Lewis gun, and in 1917 on the Somme he killed more than 20 Germans single-handed and rescued a wounded comrade under fire. This heroic conduct won him the Victoria Cross and the rank of Sergeant. He was badly wounded just before the Armistice, and died of his wounds in 1924, aged 27.

The Bluecoat School: The Boys Charity School was founded in 1706, to provide the orphan boys of Sheffield with a home and an education. From 1710 to 1911 they were housed in a building at the corner of East Parade and Campo Lane. The premises became cramped as the number of boys grew, and their only playground was the churchyard. The school had acquired land on Psalter Lane in 1796, which was let out for stone quarrying. Finally in 1911 the quarries were filled in, this fine building was erected and the boys moved to their new home.

It was known as the Blue Coat School, from the uniform of blue tailcoat with brass buttons, green corduroy trousers, white neckbands and blue muffin caps. This picture of the Charity Boys was taken in 1918. The arrow shows young George Hampshire, who had come to the school at the age of six when his father died, and who later wrote an account of the joys and hardships of his life there under the strict semi-military discipline of those days. In 1939 the school was requisitioned by the Army for a transport depot, and is now part of the Art College.

The Brincliffe Quarries in 1853: The quarries on Brincliffe Hill, of which records exist as early as 1664, produced the stone used to build most houses in Nether Edge and Sharrow. The quarry in the foreground was on land belonging to the Boys Charity School, where their new school was built in 1911. Psalter Lane crosses the picture in the middle distance. This very ancient track was almost certainly the Salters' Lane, used by pack horses to bring salt across the Peak from Cheshire. However the Salt Box Cottages, also seen here, took their name from their curious shape. They were demolished in 1967 although the rock outcrop which formed the rear walls is still standing and the sockets for floor joists are clearly visible.

The Manor House: The building shown in this picture stood in Oakdale Road. It was built some time after 1851, as a villa residence, but the earliest reference we can find is in the 1887 directory when Walter G. Parkin, glass and china merchant, appears as the occupant. Although it stood close to the site of Upper Edge farm, this house was not built from part of it; it may, however, have used the old buildings as stables. The right hand half of the house was built in this century.

Fountside: The Manor House was demolished about 1961. Today only its gate posts and the ponds survive as part of the Fountside flats, which were built by Longden's in 1967 and are one of the more inspired recent developments in our area. Incidentally, John Richdale of Richdale's Brewery lived at No. 7 Oakdale Road, and it is rumoured that his initials are incorporated in the mosaic hall flooring. The original "JR"?

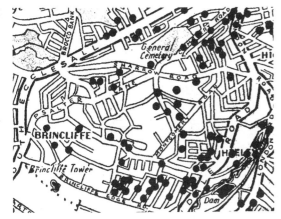

Where the bombs fell: This rather inaccurate 'official' map shows where at least some of the bombs fell on Sharrow and Nether Edge on the nights of December 12/13th and 15/16th 1940.

Nether Edge at War: When German planes swept over Sheffield at 7.00 p.m. on December 12th 1940, it was a clear frosty night with a brilliant moon. The first raiders dropped fire bombs, and soon buildings were blazing on Chelsea Road, Westbrook Bank and at Nether Edge Hospital. Here the medical supplies store caught fire and burnt fiercely for hours, acting as a beacon for the next wave of planes who came in to drop their loads of high explosives across Nether Edge and Sharrow. The blitz raged for eight hours, and when the All Clear sounded at 4.00 a.m. a terrible devastation had resulted.

There were three direct hits on the Hospital. One tore out the side of a ward killing five patients and leaving the rest lying shocked in their beds on the edge of a gaping hole until they were rescued by nurses and soldiers. Many medical supplies were lost, and this picture shows the desolate scene next morning in one of the store rooms.

In the maternity block, Mrs. Evelyn O'Brien was in labour, and could not be moved to shelter. The midwives put her under the bed, to give her some protection against flying glass and falling debris, and her son Barry was born there.

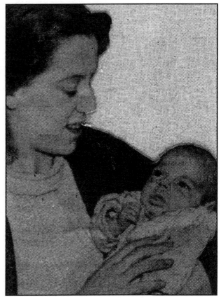

The Barrage Balloon: No, this is *not* Nether Edge! Since no picture survives of our own barrage balloon which flew from the tennis courts behind the Nether Edge Hall, here is a similar balloon at Crookesmoor. In the early days RAF men flew the balloons, but from autumn 1941 to D-Day, the Nether Edge site was entirely manned by girls of the WAAF. The sergeant, corporal and ten aircraftwomen were billeted in Nether Edge Hall, and every morning they drilled in Glen Road. Work on the balloons was physically very hard, but what the sergeant (now Mrs. Hilda Pearce of Dronfield) remembers best is the tremendous spirit of comradeship and achievement among the girls of the crew.

Cherrytree Flats: When compared to the cottages on page 5 (which were demolished to make way for this drab and graceless development) the case for conservation pressure groups needs no further comment. Such opposition as there was at the time was swept aside by our 'masters' at the Town Hall. Had the Neighbourhood Group been in existence at this time the end result might well have been different.

Ferrie's Shop: Not all the damage to our buildings was caused by the war - developers, planners and the local council have much to answer for. This small house and shop (which stood opposite Sharrow St. John's on Sharrow Lane) was, in its prime, one of our more outstanding Victorian buildings with its wealth of interesting architectural detail. It was demolished by the council in 1968 when the Washington Road flats were built. Above the right hand door were the initials "W.M." standing for Walter Mitchell, the surgeon and chemist who built the shops with George Roberts (a contractor) in 1881.

In recent times our Victorian heritage has been savaged and the character of the city centre almost erased. To resist this council-sponsored threat to our district, the Nether Edge Neighbourhood Group was formed in 1973 and has since been instrumental in preventing the wholesale redevelopment of the area.

Cherry Tree Common

The photograph shows part of a small complex of dwellings, the first of which was built in 1765, at the junction of Union Road and Cherry Tree Road. It was demolished in 1971 and replaced by Cherry Tree Common Sheltered housing opposite theUnion Hotel.

Acknowledgements:

We are indebted to the following for allowing us to reproduce their material:
Miss Freda S. Bennett – p.41 (Clifford School); Mr. W.E. Brown – p.39 bottom; Mr. M. Chaytor of Sharrow Mills – pp.30 bottom, 31; Mr. M. P. Clapham – p.37; Mrs Howe pp.10, 11 bottom; Laycock Engineering Co. Ltd. – p.36 bottom: Mr. B. Loosemore – p.41 (Arnold Loosemore V.C); Nether Edge Bowling Club – p.22; Mrs. Honor Proctor – picture of Mary Walton; Giles Robinson – pp.8,20,26, 27 top, 28 bottom, 29 top; Joe Robinson – p.46 bottom; Mr. Roe – pp.34 top; 35 top; Sheffield City Libraries – Map, pp.4,5,9,11,12 bottom, 13, 14 top, 21, 23, 24 bottom, 25, 28 top, 30 top, 32, 33, 35 bottom, 38, 39 top, 40, 42, 43, 44 top, 45, 46 top, 48; Director of Libraries & Information Services, Archives Division – pp.10 (Fairbanks Sketch) 17, 18, 19; Department of Planning & Design – pp.6, 12 top; Sheffield Newspapers – p.45; J. Edward Vickers – p.15; Malcolm Weston – pp.16 bottom, 29 bottom, 34 bottom, 41 (Miss Slater), 44 bottom; Mrs. White p.24 top; T.& J.Hale – pp.7, 14 bottom, 16 top, 26 bottom, 27 bottom, 36 top.

Back cover, David Ludham, Front Cover both sides & back inside cover Tony Venables

Woodside House, Brincliffe Edge Road, from a drawing by Henry Tatton, about 1900.

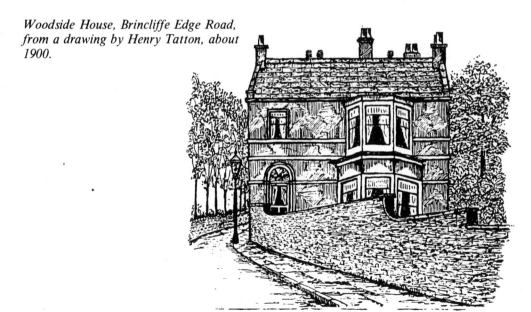

Other Nether Edge Neighbourhood Group Publications, all £4.95

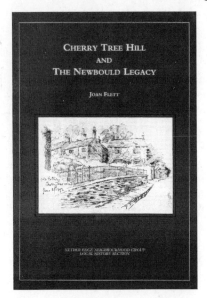

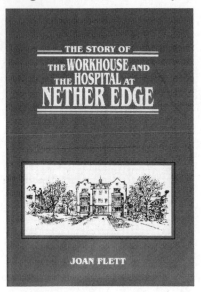

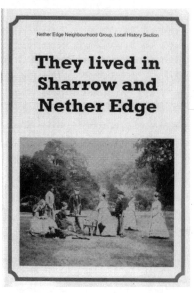

Cherry Tree Hill and the Newbould Legacy - by Joan Flett, Nether Edge Neighbourhood Group Local History Section

Published in 1999 and typeset by The Hallamshire Press. Traces the development of the Kingfield Road, St Andrew's Road, Osborne Rd, Cherry Tree Rd and Meadowbank Avenue area from 1614 to present day; from rural area with farmers carrying on a cutlery trade as a cottage industry to residential suburb; and details wills and inventories of local residents.

The Story of the Workhouse and the Hospital at Nether Edge - by Joan Flett

First published in 1985, 2nd edition 2002 which concludes by predicting its future change of use:-

'The completed project creates the biggest possible contrast to the original purpose of the site. From a place dreaded by the sick and poor, where families were separated, to luxurious family homes in an attractive tree-lined complex.'

They Lived in Sharrow and Nether Edge - a miscellany by the Nether Edge Neighbourhood Group Local History section.
First published in 1988 and republished, by popular request in 2000.

Details some of the famous - and the not so famous - residents of Nether Edge and their houses, including George Wostenholm who in 1835 started buying land in the vicinity of Cherry Tree Hill to build himself a country residence (Kenwood). He later employed Robert Marnock and Thomas Steade to develop a middle class residential area around his new home.

Other related local books by ALD

£6.95

£4.95